From The I

Copyright © R

Firs

Published by

All rights reserved. Without limiting the rights under copyright reserved above, no part of this publication may be reproduced, stored in or introduced into a database and retrieval system or transmitted in any form or any means (electronic, mechanical, photocopying, recording or otherwise) without the prior written permission of both the owner of copyright and the above publishers.

Printed by Create Space

From The Inside Of The Mirror

K .P. Morrison, Richard

ISBN-13: 978-1484961674

ISBN-10: 1484961676

Dedication

Dedicated to all of our nations heroes both alive and gone.

Special Thanks

I want to first thank everyone who has been in my corner for their continued support. I want to thank my mother for always being there, and my father for being so honest I also want to thank "Ma", and the complete staff at Seaford Young Marines.

Semper Fi

Authors Note

The Seaford Young Marines are a unit of the national program based out of Seaford, Delaware. They have made large jumps to success in the short time that they have been around. Teaching leadership, teamwork, and discipline, they have a large positive influence on several local youth. They have had a large influence on me in making me the person I am today. I support this program fully, and ask everyone to go check them out at

http://www.seafordyoungmarines.com/

Unit Commander - Sean Morrison

Unit XO - Shawn Hines

Unit Adjutant - Liza Morrison

And so it begins...............

Uncover The Mask

Most curious for you to ask,

Who am I?

Did you say?

Since you ask, I'll drop my mask.

First of I'm a boy,

Which I'm sure my looks display.

And yes I am a teen,

That much easily seen.

Marine Corps Brat, and true is that,

Always Faithful, salute to that.

To others a musician, an athlete.

Lower still a smarty pant tart,

Lastly, yes it's true, I am a poet.

And by golly, I surely know it,

Yet I'm covered by a mask until I show it.

"So many people are seen in only one way. Think about in school, you have the jocks, the band kids, the nerds etc. Yet, people are not one dimensional. There is so much you will never know about people until you get to know them. A lot of times someone shows different sides to different groups of people. Even deeper it's not uncommon for people to have skills or hobbies, no one even knows about. They hold them close, they shield them. No one will ever see them unless they take off the mask they use as cover."

Dedicated to my mask remover's

Unknown Soldier

Who are you?

How did you die?

Is it true? Or did they lie?

Did you die for me? Was it for liberty?

Regardless I'll say thank you.

I mean it, it's true.

You gave it all in a distant land,

Rising strong together we stand.

In remembrance we bow our heads,

Our hearts heavy, filled with lead.

The tears they fall from our eyes,

As we all join and cry.

Red white and blue, Behind me fly's,

Thanks to you it still flies.

The Unknown Soldier.

"Throughout the history of our great country, several brave men and women have stood in defense of our nation. Unfortunately, not all the people we send overseas come back with a name. Some of these heroes remain unknown. There are several monuments, to the unknown heroes, from several different eras' ranging from the revolutionary war to the war on terrorism of the present."

Dedicated to the heroes unknown.

Just Like a Bird

I wish I had wings,

Just like a bird.

I wish my voice could sing,

Just like a bird.

I wish I could be,

Just like a bird.

And especially free,

Just like a bird.

"Sometimes it feels like we as humans, are stuck in a revolving door, we can't get out of. The door spins and spins and the same views go round and round. Sometimes it would be nice to have the ability to fly anywhere we wanted when we wanted, and to just be free."

Dedicated to all the caged Birds

Not Rich

I have tons of gold,

And own all once sold.

Every Car, Every Game,

I earned through my fame.

But then why do I cry?

I'll be honest, disregard the lies.

Something is missing.

No love, even with my wishing.

No loving friends, or family,

Nope me alone just me.

I may have all the money.

But being rich does not mean money.

"What makes someone rich? This idea has been turned over and over for thousands of years. Everywhere from the bible, to Ancient Greek legends of king Midas. Me, I think money has nothing to do with happiness. I think to truly be rich is to have love. A life without love is a sad thing."

Dedicated to all those who make me rich.

Moons

Moons bright,

Twinkles light,

Gentle glow,

Tears flow.

Bright eyes,

Made me smile,

All worth the while.

Moved the tides,

Moved my heart,

The moons.

"The moon has captivated humanity from the beginning of time. The bright light it shines at night was a comfort to some in there darkest hours. The moon has the power to shine light, when its wants or it can shell up and hide."

Dedicated to the keeper of the moons.

My Turn

Storms will brew,

Fires will burn.

I won't be blue,

For it is my turn.

I will be strong,

Of this I am sure.

I will last long,

For I'll be pure.

I will keep going,

For the ones I love.

Loved ones proving,

I'll fly like a dove.

Storms will brew,

Fires will burn.

I won't be blue,

For it is my turn.

"Sometimes it feels like we just keep getting smacked. It's like every time you go to take your turn someone jumps in front of you. So what should you do? Lean on those who care for you, your family, your friends, eventually, you'll get your turn."

Dedicated to those I lean on.

Sea

A blue sea,

A place full of glee.

Fish swim by,

Ahead birds fly.

Endless life,

No one's strife.

To be alive,

This I strive.

To be endless,

Without the mess.

Sea sized big,

Through fog I dig,

To find how to be,

The sea.

"The sea is such a symbolic thing. It has been used in poetry and music for centuries. For me the sea is a place of peace, something I've been around my whole life. Everyone has a paradise, mine is the sea."

Dedicated to my fellow space rocket hero.

Load

Down a long road,

A wise man walks.

Carrying a load,

To no one he talks.

He carries peace,

A hater of war.

He wishes to cease,

All that can harm,

He walks along that road,

With his load,

That his burden is to carry.

"Although worldwide, peace is highly unlikely to ever happen, it is a nice idea. An idea strived for by some people, they try to be slow to temper, quick to forgive, and most of all kind to the world."

Dedicated to my friend the bohemian.

Freedom Is Not Free

In recent events, it's clear to me,

That freedom indeed is not free.

Brave ones sent to defend our ways,

Sacrifices are made but missed in the haze.

Fighting for liberty, justice, the American life,

They fight on, risking their life.

Birthdays, Holidays, Family, they miss them all.

Yet everyday there again stand tall.

As for those who gave it all,

I hold most deep in my heart.

They answered to their country's call.

Away from home, away they go.

So again, I must say,

Freedom is not free.

"Millions have died, for the freedoms we enjoy every day. They won't get to see their kids grow up, or their siblings graduate, or any of the other things we look forward to. They are gone; they gave all in defense of us. So I challenge you to try and remember these heroes. It's the least we can do, Let them live on in our hearts."

Dedicated to America's POW, MIA, and KIA.

Daily Cycle

Red sky, above does fly,

The sun sets on another day.

The owls let out that distant cry,

Ending another day of May.

The lake glistens, with the fleeing sun,

The world spins slowly to night,

The sun and moon, the race they run,

Ahhh, the beautiful celestial sight.

The day rises with the sun of the east,

The creatures rise with the glow.

The birds rise for the wormy east,

As the earth carry's on turning slow.

"The cycle of day and night, is a grand part of mother earth. It is a magnificent thing, which is rarely recognized with the craziness of daily life. Take a second to realize how much it affects our habits and the things we do."

Dedicated to Mother Earth.

Purple Flowers

Purple Flowers,

Grow in my mind,

Behind answers,

I try to find.

I watch my garden,

As it burns,

I am the warden,

Of these ferns.

Flowers I water,

Every day,

There I loiter,

Funny to say.

For this is my mind,

With purple flowers,

Behind answers, I try to find.

"I think everyone has things they wish they could erase from their minds. Things they wish they never had to see again. Sometimes instead of trying to change the past it is best to just move on. Let the past go, move on. If you're stuck in the past, you will most likely miss your present."

Dedicated to the Past.

Rainbows

In my life's wonder,

I have the rainbows.

In all the bitter,

When it's dark they glow.

They glow so bright,

In all the muck.

Seven different lights,

Oh beautiful luck.

My friends,

My personal rainbows.

Till the end,

The rainbows.

"Have you ever met someone, who was extremely quirky, and a little on the odd side? I am sure most everyone has. Me personally I have met several people like this. The difference is though, I love these people. No matter how bad something is they make it better with the pure way they glow."

Dedicated to my Quirky Rainbow Friends.

Free

A surplus of emotion,

My minds revolution.

From anger I now fly,

An old danger I pass by.

The hate I once let grip me,

I've let it go for I could be.

I've risen against madness,

Glistening tears of joy.

Now I am free,

Free as can be.

I've broken the chains,

Trudged through the rains.

With the anger gone,

I am free to move on.

"Anger is such a nasty emotion; it can literally kill you by raising blood pressure and a number of other health issues. If you hold onto anger at someone, you're giving that person control over you. So if you can find a way to let go, Joy is way more rewarding than anger."

Dedicated to all the Grumpy Bears.

Looking In the Mirror

Across the meadow,

I see you there.

Your head hung low,

At you I stare.

Your eyes run wild,

Your crooked teeth pointed.

To you I must look mild,

Standing here so self-appointed.

Through your eyes, I see your mind,

The fear, the hate, the tears.

And with horror, I come to find,

I was gazing in a mirror.

"A mirror is a simple thing in reality. It reflects, what's in front of it, without a care of feelings or hurting anyone. If you want to know who you are look at your reflection."

Dedicated to those who tell the truth?

See the Sun

Every day I see the sun,

Joy springs up in my chest.

My happiness goes for a run,

And I feel my best.

Every day I see the sun,

You make me smile.

My life goes on a run,

And it all worth the while.

"The sun is the center of our solar system. Our world revolves around it, and everything is content. Find the things and people you love, make them your sun, and then even when the sun won't shine your life will be bright."

Dedicated to the pieces of my sun.

Time

Tick Tock,

Goes the clock.

One thing,

That never stops,

Time.

Tick Tock,

Decisions,

Religions,

Our world,

Full of differences.

Tick Tock,

We are united,

Through Time.

"The cultures and ideas are so different from culture to culture. The things we as Americans enjoy, is considered to be boring or useless in other countries. Yet no matter how different we all are, one thing affects everybody. That thing is time."

Dedicated to the old men, and how things used to be.

I Am a Man

Yes I wear glasses,

And yes I am over weight.

I may be different from the masses,

But why can't I be great?

I tried to be your friend,

But you punched me.

So that didn't work out in the end,

Now it's easy to see,

Just how great I am.

I don't have to be a bully,

To prove that I am a man.

"So many kids are bullied nowadays. In some kids it lowers their self-esteem, and even causes depression. Yet for some kids, it makes them strong. It teaches them about perseverance and it shows them just how AWESOME they are."

Dedicated to all the Bullied.

Suicide's Beast

Evil Beast,

On pain,

It feasts,

Lives' it drains.

Deadly tool,

Called depression.

Thrives on foolish thought,

Life's recession.

Burns through glee,

Try and plea,

To stiff a fee,

I beg you'll see.

Don't take the offer,

Denied the ride,

Avoid your coffer,

Pray you'll hide,

From the beast,

The beast called,

Suicide.

Suicide is a monstrous infestation. It's an idea that seeps into someone's mind when there most vulnerable. It takes their lives and causes extreme grief in a family. Suicide is a monster."

Dedicate to Big Mike.

Hero

The word hero is overused.

Great singers and athletes not,

That word so largely abused.

Heroes are not all rich with yachts.

Heroes are ready to give it all.

In the front they stand,

Waving liberty's flag so tall.

Defending the homeland,

The family's you and me.

They master the fear.

Bravery be it the key,

As they are sent off with tears.

Our protectors,

Our heroes.

"What is a hero? Some people will name off great athletes, or singers, and even famous actors. In my opinion a hero is someone with the bravery to do what not all could. The paramedics, police, fireman, and the military. These are the ones who deserve to be praised as heroes."

Dedicated to our nation's First Responders.

Birth of Poetry

In the hall of Mercury in Rome,

My hobby was born.

The lord came to the temple his home.

His mind mixed, his thoughts torn,

How was he to spread the word?

He wrote his mind, his message.

At that he gave the scroll to a bird.

The bird found Apollo waiting on the edge.

Apollo took the words, adding his rhyme.

The music accompanied inside every line.

The word was spread in due time,

Poetry was born and that was just fine.

"Poetry has been around for ages. It can be found everywhere. It's in music, in advertising, even in our own minds. Poetry is always there in your hearts, just waiting to be grabbed."

Dedicated to my favorite Poet in hopes to avoid Troy together.

People Watching

Out of all the things to watch in nature,

People themselves bestow the most wonder.

The pace they move, the way they walk.

The words they say, the style they talk.

The look in their eyes, the way they gaze.

The way they live in their daily days.

All are clues, with a story to tell.

They are the clues that shout and yell.

Just be calm and sit and you will see,

Someone's story maybe it will be me.

"One of the most interesting things to see is other people. We as a species are so different from one to another. What I am like is more than likely very different from you. The world is a story and each of us is a point of view."

Dedicated to my Father, and Friend

Chase

A beast chases prey,

It can never catch.

Every single day,

Trying to fetch.

He scared it away,

It left,

The chase is on,

Day and night,

The beast chases,

Bright or no light,

He races.

Mistakes made,

Slow him down.

He is so afraid,

To look like a clown.

He loves his prey,

He will eternally chase,

For this is a most,

Important race.

"We all have dreams. Some of us chase them, and others just go through life wishing for change. The ones who chase there dream, have a long road ahead. Yet if you refuse to give up, and live with determination, anything is possible."

Dedicated to the chasers.

Mama Bear

The fear,

The drain,

The pain,

The tears,

Mama Bear cures all.

"Mothers are wonderful people, at least most are. No matter how bad the world seems, Mom is there. When you need someone to lean on, they are there."

Dedicated to my Mama Bear.

Gas Out

I met a girl,

Beautiful smart and bubbly.

She gave my stomach a twirl,

I thought I had to pee.

Then I got cramps,

And almost threw up.

I asked her out,

She said yes,

Good lord it was a blessing,

To finally let the gas out.

"I do not know how it is for others, but me I get nervous. The more you like someone the more awkward it seems. Awkwardness affects everyone different. For some it causes gas, it must truly suck for them."

Dedicated to all the gassers.

My Dear

My Dear, My Dear,

Tis thee I love.

My Dear, My Dear,

Thy purest dove.

My Love, My Love,

Give the world to you.

My Love, My Love,

My word rings true.

For you, for you,

I'll give it all.

For you, for you,

Give me a reason to,

Stand tall.

"Poetry and love have been partners since the beginning of each. Love is the feeling with poetry being its written word of expression. The Greeks wrote of Aphrodite, and the Romans wrote of Venus. Love has seeped its way into poetry, and poetry is happy to receive it. It has been this way in all of history, and will probably stay this way as long as humanity lives."

    Dedicated to the true writer of Love.

The Star

In the most distant reaches of outer space,

There sits a star shining mellow.

It's wonderful presence shown on my face,

It sits in a system of which no one knows.

The light it shines seen only to me,

My love being that star, be it my obsession.

When it comes to the world that is the key.

I must find it and conquer it, to win,

It sits there mocking me, be I its servant?

Is it my master, my king, my ruler?

I try with force to ruin its tint.

Yet my advances, at will it deters.

That heavenly sphere, of which I'll rule.

I will control, I will earn.

I must, I must, less it makes me a fool,

For together, ultimately we both burn.

"Each and every one of us has that one trait. That one trait of our character that has the ability to ruin us. A lot of times that trait id two faced. In some ways it might help you get farther in life. Then on the other side, it has the ability to be the ruin of everything you work for. Yet if we can control, these parts, of ourselves we can be the most powerful, talented forms of ourselves. Just like all else in life you need to find a happy medium."

Dedicated to the overcoming of one's self.

Fly

Me I would love to fly,

Above the clouds I could shout so loud.

I would be free, that no one can deny,

I would use the power to remove my shroud.

The world spread, underneath me,

Earth spread out for all to see.

If only I could fly,

The world would be mine,

If only I could fly,

Everything would be fine.

"The ultimate freedom, the ability to fly. It would be a magnificent thing to be able to see the world, from the sky above. We could see just how small the small everyday quarrels are compared to the big picture. We as humans could release the day to day stress and set ourselves free."

Dedicated to all the knowledge us as humans miss.

Love

Love is wise,

Love is free.

When all is blind,

Love can see.

Love is kind,

Love is strong.

Life is short,

But love is long.

Love is smart,

Love is brave.

Love it flows,

Just like the waves.

Love is great,

"Love" being the tower.

And with them,

It grows by the hour.

"Weddings are quite intriguing events. They represent the merging of two families into one. Sometime the families are like two opposing sides waiting to attack each other. And other times the families come together perfectly to form one new family that is stronger merged."

Dedicated to the summer of 2013 weddings.

Dream

I feel my inner fire,

The flame crackles and roars.

The world, my love, my home,

The soothing voice of joy.

In my body thou harmony sings,

In a feverish pitch most coy.

Screaming, buzzing, pierce it rings,

The music of my life moves.

The pound for pound of the travels,

The sound of those thousand hooves,

As my weary state starts to unravel.

The world shifts to my norm,

I awaken from the tranquil seam.

I find myself safe and warm,

In my bed, I lie after my dream.

"A dream is an amazing thing; it shows us things that we know without knowing. It opens our mind to the things we think without thinking. A dream can be a guide, or a jailer. It can lead you or torture you. A dream can be whatever it wants to be and we just have to deal with them. I find that most interesting."

Dedicated to the sleepers imagination.

Strings

I strum my pick so light,

It lets out that beautiful sound.

Faster now with the string I fight,

"Out, out chords" I scream and pound.

Screech by screech, learn guitar.

The strings snap and break,

I strummed too hard.

Fight and fight till strings go break,

Try and try, try again.

Guitar I will learn,

I just don't know when.

"Anyone who has gone through the ordeal of learning guitar will understand this. When trying to learn guitar, it is as if you are fighting with it sometimes, but when you do learn, you receive a great award."

Dedicated to the art of music.

Tears

Some tears are blue,

Some are red.

Pain of the mind,

Pain of the body.

Both will hurt,

Both will suck.

Tears of red,

Tears of Blue.

Bleeding from the cuts,

Wet crying eyes.

Caused by fights,

Caused by lies.

Blue tears mind,

Red tears blood,

Tears we cry.

Tears of red,

Tears of blue,

Tears we cry,

Me and you.

"Throughout life, things will knock us down. The tears are it red or blue represents the release of that which is bad. We bleed to let out the bad infections, and we cry to let out our pain"

Dedicated to the men who can cry."

Change

I am change,

I can be great.

You all will see,

What I can be.

To change this world,

Start with yourself.

All ideas twirled,

Find one's self.

Follow your values,

Follow what's right.

Hold friends tight,

As you watch the hues.

The hues of good,

Watch them flood.

Every street,

On swift feet.

The world can be happy,

Wash out the darks.

Wash away all that harks,

Finally eternally happy.

Just watch it flow,

The change you made,

Started with you.

You can glow.

What I can be,

You all will see.

You all will see,

I can be great.

I am change.

"This is a simple idea of mine I hold close. I do not believe one person can cause global peace or worldwide Love. Yet isn't one person doing good things a small change then if they did nothing? Isn't a small change in the right direction better than nothing?"

Dedicated to the great peace seekers.

Bubble

So much pain,

Let it rain.

Out a new lane,

Let it go.

Put it in a bubble,

Clean out the rubble.

Worries float away,

Have a better day.

Put it in a bubble,

Clean out the rubble.

Worries float away,

Have a better day.

Thank you Mr. Bubble,

Take away my worries.

So I won't be sorry,

I'll put them in a bubble.

"I don't know what caused me to write this. Yet I do like the idea of it, when something is stressful just put it in a little bubble and let it float away with your stress."

Dedicated to Mrs. K

<u>We All Grow</u>

We all grow,

Energy flows,

Life goes on.

We all start as fawns,

We start as seeds,

Fighting through weeds.

We grow tall,

Away from the walls.

We get stronger,

And better,

And brighter,

And bolder.

We all grow,

Energy flows,

Life goes on,

We all grow.

"We all start off small, weak, and feeble. Both mentally and physically. As we go through life we get stronger, from the things we learn and the things we do. Everything that ever happens to us makes us stronger. That is the beauty of the human race to me."

Dedicated to the monster's baby.

Passed Us By

She and I were there in that most tranquil place,

The sun on her face as she held me tight,

Not a care, not a fear to fight.

My head on her shoulder feeling so safe,

Heavy like a boulder I slip into sleep,

Heavy dreams shook by the distant storm.

RUN, RUN from the storm,

As we got up to leave,

A smile my face heaves.

For joy followed her and I,

As time passed us by.

"Some of our most vivid memories, are the ones that define us. The world we have been a part of is our own. Our own little worlds starring us, ignorant of the real comings and goings around us."

Dedicated to the defining of humanity.

High Sky Free

Freedom,

Vacation,

Ultimatum,

Of no relation.

Beautiful sun,

Free I run,

Broke my cage,

In my rage.

I am free,

Of all the stress.

I will be without, distress.

Free I fly,

High I rise,

To the sky's.

Free I'll be, You'll all see,

This is me.

"Sometimes, we are like birds scared to fly. It is as if our wings were injured and it is too scary to try and fly again. A lot of times when this is the case, the best way to cure the fear is to just spread those wings and fly."

Dedicated to the spreading of wings.

Loving Sea

A lovely sea,

Roams in my head.

On the tracks I be,

As I come to my new stead.

This is where I live.

Anything I'd give,

To hold onto this moment.

In all so sweet,

Life's great treats.

Forever, my head I rest,

In this place the best.

The lovely sea,

I have come to see.

"The people closest most often are the ones we push away. Yet when we try and come back, the ones who truly care are there, open arms and smile abroad. It is a great feeling to realize what you didn't."

Dedicated to my parents who waited.

Blue Sky

Shadows creep,

Demons reap.

Light shines through,

The sky is blue.

Hope always brought,

By the blue in the sky.

The twinkling eyes,

Of loved ones.

Sometimes a cloud,

Covers the sun.

Thunder so loud,

You want to run.

Tears be shed,

Pain we've bled,

But light shines through,

The sky is blue.

"Things are not always happy in life. We will get knocked down and pushed around by life. We will see rainy days. After every storm, just give it time the beautiful blue sky will shine again".

Dedicated to the people of my sky.

Moon's 2

Moon's bright,

Twinkling lights.

In your glow,

My tears flow.

The winner of the sacred race,

When I see thy face,

My heart starts to race.

Bright lovely light shines,

Through all of the dark's twine.

They Moved the tides,

The ocean's glide,

Making mind smart,

Renewing my heart.

The Moon's Bright,

Twinkling lights.

"Things change, just like while working on this book, my opinion of the moon has changed. Instead of removing the original poem, I just added this one. For why should I hide that just like all of our kind, my opinions can change".

Dedicated to the Holder of the Moons.

Here's Another Tear

You're gone,

Not here.

I'm Alone,

Here's another tear.

I miss you,

I love you.

Now I fear,

Here's another tear.

You left so fast,

In the past, Now I see.

Life is hard,

Without you near.

Life is so hard,

So here is another tear.

"I was fortunate enough to have a lot of grandparents, not a part of my bloodline. Yet even though our blood was different, love made a bond that kept us close. This is dedicated to my earliest memory of watching one slip from our realm to live with god".

Dedicated to the mother of the small woods at the poplar circus.

A Dog's Smart

Some say dogs are dumb,

I call that a statement bum.

When they have to pee,

They pee.

When they have to itch,

They itch.

When they want to eat,

They eat.

When they want to play,

They play.

With all of this in mind,

It is easy to find,

Dogs are quite smart!

"I love dogs. They are very instinctive animals. Unlike humans, who are structured by the rules of humanity, they are free. Their judgment is not misguided based on others opinions the ways ours are. So with that alone I feel dogs are the smartest of all earths' creatures."

Dedicated to Beo, Princess and the cat that wishes it was a dog.

Boston Street

I saw a man on the street,

Head hung low, Shuffling his feet.

His demeanor that of a taken blow,

I asked of his burden, and what was wrong,

Asking why he looked so glum.

He started a story long.

And I quote

"I thought it a drum,

Celebration of the race.

My wife running up,

Joy to horror changed her face.

She fell, Gone!, She didn't get up!

Cowards, Cowards! Took my wife!

Those bombs, That coward tool,

It ended my wife's life."

I sat with that man all day,

Trying to comfort him in every way.

He got up shuffling his feet,

Down that sunny Boston Street.

"April 13th 2013, America, was again tested. Cowards tried to strike fear into the people. Yet again just like we always have, and always will America still stands tall. Let freedom be heard over every continent. Let all feel the power of liberty, and most of all let freedom ring."

Dedicated to all the victims of terror worldwide.

Pete

Little Pete brave and true,

Joined the navy to sail the blue.

Stationed in a harbor littered with pearls,

Flirting and loving the island girls.

Laughing and working, without a care,

Till a horrible day, to expect he would not dare.

The Japs came low, guns blazing,

Miles away smoke seen raising.

Pete was cleaning the big ships Galley,

Hearing shots from a fight he couldn't see.

Pete pounded so hard as she sunk,

All went jolting and flipping,

As the ship went dipping.

The divers, they heard him pound,

To save him, the mission to which they were bound.

Then silent he fell,

While the water made his lungs swell.

Every year on Pearl Harbor day,

Join with me, together let's say,

A prayer for Pete, and the island navy,

Peace against the fate they had to meet.

"I had the honor of performing with a Mass band at Pearl Harbor in the year of 2011. I saw something there that has had a large effect on me to this very day. God Bless America."

Dedicated to those forever in the ship.

Ending to Beginnings

Is there a true end,

This I ask my dear friend.

When one shows over,

On comes another.

When a story's read,

You just go and tread,

And start all over.

So my dear friend,

Does anything ever end?

I must say this singing,

Ends mark beginnings.

"When something is finished or completed there is always more to do. Just like now that this book is finished, hopefully another will be not far behind."

Dedicated to future possibilities.

WAIT READ ON!

Ahead is the preview for my upcoming Novel "Squeezed By Shadows"

An inside look at depression in teens.

March

3/21/12

10:36 P.M.

What is it about spring that brings so much joy? Spring in being a season, is nothing but a title. Yet I wonder about the source of all this happiness. Some may say the warmth, and the color emerging from the depths of the spinning rock we titled earth. Yet all the hues are doomed to fade into the vast greyness cast by the pure evil that emits from humanity. Then right next to the color, the warmth will fade away into the mist pushed by the pure force of a human's cold heart.

This dreaded thing given to me by Mrs. Kay is useless. What good is a book to write about my feelings? Yet isn't it the job of a guidance counselor to be useless? They teach of feelings and how to cope, but who really listens? Alas Mrs. Kay is a kind enough lady so I agreed, I'll write in this empty book until it is full. Then I can be done, and leave it in a closet to collect dust like every other menial thing created by man. For what worth do my feelings really hold?

My day was like any other. You walk through those large doors into the battlefield of adolescence; you have all the different factions of the young community. The jocks, snobs, rednecks, rich kids, poor kids, geeks, and then separated from all, me. I walked along the undrawn lines, of war to my little nest of a corner in the commons area. There as usual I sat until the piercing sound of the bell rang through my bones. Getting up slowly to draw no attention to myself I made my way to my first class.

My first class of the day was math, which is nothing more than an opportunity to give the over analytical a chance to teach something. Of course with it being the way the world works, I'm great at math, but I don't enjoy it. How could I? You sit there doing equations and formulas that have no power in the workings of our world. As usual I flew through the work like it was meant for the supremely stupid, which includes the majority of my peers.

The silence was destroyed by the sharp ring of the phone. As usual everyone looked around nervous, like ants under a magnifying glass. For what is scarier to a teen then the office calling your class? The teacher did the normal blank stare at the students, lost in the dialogue he spoke. Then his eyes swept the room to find the target of the Administrative call. Searching, searching, searching, me?

  The teacher pointed like I was a caged animal and he said my name slow as if I was stupid. "Anthony Lee Drake". Of course he said my full name. I hate my name, he couldn't just say Tony. No it is definitely easier and timelier to say it all.

  He went on to tell me Mrs. Kay wanted me in her office, which led to the mocking sneers of my fellow students. I got up readying my mind for the onslaught any counselor would make for someone as normal as me.

As much as I hate counselors, I truly do like Mrs. Kay, she is one of those people who seemed to genuinely care for others. She has that rosiness of her cheeks, shining through her tan skin, accentuated by a slightly round face all framed by a short cut of curly brown ringlets. Her features bare a direct insight to her personality, soft and warm, with a small dash of sassy.

I walked to her office, with my eyes pointed at my feet. Isn't it funny how such small platforms, can lift and move a body along? That idea is so unbelievable to me, yet there it was. It is things like that, which frustrate me. The things so illogical that work when they shouldn't, but isn't the very existence of humanity an anomaly? A race born out of scientific mistakes, are we any more than that?

When I looked up, I was standing at the door, eyes locked on the plaque saying counselor. The idea of someone paid to fix me or understand me, has always made me uncomfortable. For isn't that everyone's own personal goal, to understand themselves?

I walked into her office, trying to gauge those soft silent eyes. I realized that I would find nothing this way so I took my seat in the chair across from her. She sat there looking at me as if I was a puzzle to take apart, something I would have despised had it been anyone else. The only reason I actually liked Mrs. Kay was regardless that it was her job; she truly did seem to care.

Yet I was nervous about being there with her. Last time I was there the week before; she questioned me about the bruises on my arm. Yet I couldn't tell her and I still can't. Telling people would be no different than killing myself, and as miserable as I am, I don't want to die.

Yet all she said was "take this", and she handed me this very journal. I started to argue, yet she cut me off. She spoke slowly yet with a certainty to her voice. "I want you to fill this empty book, with everything you feel is important". After that she simply turned her chair to face her computer. I took that as my chance to leave.

The rest of my day was without incident. I went home on the bus, which is just a big moving arena, for the different teenage armies to fight it out, while I sit quietly alone in the back.

I got off the bus and crept into the house without letting Dave hear me. He as usual was asleep in a drunken stupor on the couch, the smell of booze, sweating from his pores. I snuck up the stairs into my room sliding onto my bed and started sleeping off the day.

I just woke up remembering Mrs. Kay's request, and being she's not that bad of a person, I decided to oblige. Although I still feel this whole thing is useless, at least now I have somewhere to rant besides my head.

3/22/13

1:04 A.M.

Waking up in the middle of the night is never fun, especially from a nightmare. The way they slide into your thought, is like a predator waiting until the dark to leap and attack. They come fast, strong and even when you awake in a panic, your body maintains the steady quiver that come's when one lives through steady fear.

As useless as this feels, I was told to write what I felt was important, and what can be more important than my worst nightmares? Is there even a more powerful force than that of fear? All mighty terror, which can bring about panic, riots, war, and in the end lead to peace? Is fear not man's greatest enemy, while maintaining itself as a mighty tool?

Yet here fear holds no goodness, no aid to me. It enters my dreams and replays the most horrid day of my existence. It shows the uniformed men, getting out of the flashing carriage, creeping up to the porch as I peer out the blinds from the second floor. I was weary of anyone for I had been alone for days, what true company was the drunk who my mother married?

The men knocked softly as if hoping no one would answer. I crept down the stairs to see, to hear, and to understand. I was wishing mother was back, she loved the hubbub that followed police. Yet mother was not here, she had not been here for days, but I knew she would arrive any moment.

They spoke softly which bore a funny contrast to Dave's typical loud grunts, he labels as speech. I heard the words without hearing them. No it was more like I heard what couldn't be true, impossible!

Then just like every other time this image attacks me, I woke up destroyed. It brings a funny feeling, one as if you are floating over boiling water, close enough to feel the heat, yet too far to finish you off, a slow and unkind torture.

Sweating, shaking, and broken I woke up like so many other nights, destroyed from living through something yet again. The same way I had lived through it every night for months. The spoken truth, I don't want to hear, Mother is gone.

3/24/12

4:31 P.M.

What is important? Isn't the idea of importance nothing more than a thing of relevance? To a dog, nothing is more important than its bone. Whereas to most of my fellow 15 year old males, nothing is more important than teenage girls. Most certainly a bone is as unimportant to me as girls are to dogs.

So this is what I feel is important enough to write to this inanimate object, as if it were a friend. I have no friends, I am alone. Much like a fish solo in its tank. I see the people around me and they see me, but there is no true interaction. Similar to the glass of the fish tank there is some sort of invisible barrier separating me from my species. Me I am alone, and this I feel is important.

3/25/13

7:19 P.M.

Why is it that I feel this way, this feeling of cold nothingness? It feels as if my soul is one of the empty fields of the Midwest, yet I am covered in ice and snow. The soil that makes me up is becoming hard and cold while air that is my heart is becoming sharp as if it in itself is the knife trying to kill me. Yet am I even alive, is being empty, truly life?

Is the world truly so cruel, that I must endure this? Do things ever get better? Or is this the sole purpose of existence, wake up every day, become more and more empty, till we die as shells with nothing inside?

Mother always so happy always so bright, spoke of the world in light. She spoke of singing birds, their voices spreading joy the way the sun's rays spread heat. An undeniable chain of cheer, spread from one being to another.

The world mother saw, while beautiful does not exist. Mother was the exact opposite of color blind, where there was no color, she saw a rainbow. Where there was no sunshine, she saw light. Even when all was grey she saw white.

Yet does any of what she saw matter? Does it matter that her world was bright? Does it matter to anyone that mine is black?

3/26/13

3:24 A.M.

    I can't sleep; it's as if my world is shifting to something I can't understand. Right now when the rest of my kind is asleep, I prowl. Looking through old photos should be a joyous thing, it's not for me. I look at the three of us, standing there like all is perfect. Yet out of all the deceitful, photos are the worst. When you go to get your photo taken you smile, regardless of who you're with. We smile every time, like it's some sort of law.

    Here in front of me lays a perfect example, me so young, so ignorant, mother, and the monster. The monster drinking the whole store up on the corner of my street. The monster that doesn't deserve life.

    The monster drinks the elixir of his strength. He acts as if no one watches, but I do. He acts as if he is alone, but I am here. The monster sleeps like he is innocent, but he is not. The monster thinks no one knows, but I do.

Coming Soon.......

Printed in Great Britain
by Amazon